D1498223

WITHDRAWN FROM
MACALESTER COLLEGE
LIBRARY

Voyages to the Inland Sea

The first of a series
on contemporary Midwest poetry

Voyages to the Inland Sea

ESSAYS AND POEMS BY

Lisel Mueller – John Knoepfle – Dave Etter

John Judson, Editor
Center for Contemporary Poetry, Murphy Library
Wisconsin State University at La Crosse. 1971

Copyright 1971 by John Judson

SBN 911462-05-8

Library of Congress catalog card 74-634578

CONTENTS

FOREWORD

The editor especially would like to thank Emerson G. Wulling and Edwin L. Hill for their expert and enthusiastic help in making this book. Both should be designated editors

Also, my thanks to Donovan Riley, who helped transform a vague hope to a definite legal and financial possibility; to William P. Vafeas, whose drawing *Voyage* inspired the title of this book and graces the titlepage; and to Robert L. Burns, who most capably cleared all previous copyrights.

—John Judson

Lisel Mueller

"Small Poem About the Hounds and the Hares" first appeared in *Poetry*.

"The Picture from China" first appeared in *Cafe Solo*.
    dencies, University of North Carolina Press, Chapel Hill, N.C.

"On Finding a Bird's Bones in The Woods" appeared in *Depen-*

"Highway 2, Illinois" first appeared in *Shenandoah*.

"A Farewell, A Welcome" first appeared in *Inside Outer Space*, edited by Robert Vas Dias, Doubleday.

*

MIDWESTERN POETRY:
GOODBYE TO ALL THAT

Lisel Mueller

1

THE IDEA OF REGIONAL POETRY seems an oddly old-fashioned one in this age, when a politician can give a speech in Philadelphia in the morning, another in Chicago in the afternoon, and address a rally in Los Angeles that evening; when, at any given time, a considerable number of women all over the country are wearing identical dresses and preparing identical frozen vegetables; when a teenager with a powerful enough transistor radio can confirm that the Top Ten in Chicago are also the Top Ten in Albuquerque and Toledo and Sudbury, Ontario — that, in fact, the rat-tat-tat of the disc jockeys is obligingly interchangeable.

Admittedly, when we speak of Midwestern poetry, we speak of something that is passing out of existence. For most young people, regional differences are already so obsolete as to be nonexistent. Of course, they acknowledge differences of landscape, but they accurately recognize differences in attitudes, speech, and customs as having more to do with age than region. We are a fluid people; the uniformity of life all over the country makes it easy for us to change houses and neighbors as we change cars and clothes. Our communal allegiances are short-lived, and why shouldn't they be, when one house, one street, one subdivision looks like any other?

All the more fitting then to take stock of what the present generation of Midwestern poets may be the last to represent: a particular tradition, a special focus, a recognizable community of feeling, which has nothing to do with a "school," since these poets are scattered and do not adhere to any common literary credo. My definition of Midwestern, for the purpose of this paper, ignores a great many poets born in this region. Surely no one associates T. S. Eliot and Hart Crane primarily with Missouri and Ohio. And San Francisco and New York rightly claim Michael McClure and Kenneth Koch, respectively, not Marysville, Kansas, and Cincinnati, Ohio. I am also arbitrarily excluding those poets whose concerns and imagery are exclusively urban. All large cities in this country are very similar; at least they share a great many more physical and cultural characteristics with each other than with their particular hinterlands. It has been fifty-four years since Carl Sandburg celebrated Chicago as an expanding, overgrown frontier town, and by now the shoe no longer fits.[1]

What I am left with by way of definition is a body of poetry that owes its life to the heart of the heartland: the vast stretches of farmland, the rolling hills with their many shades of green, the great rivers and thousands of small lakes, the forests of Michigan, Minnesota, and Wisconsin, the towns with their rectangular layouts, their elm-shaded porches, their Elks' Clubs, and their dreary Main Streets. Ultimately, it owes its life to a population of 19th century settlers, predominantly Protestant, predominantly British, German, and Scandinavian, whose society was founded on such principles as egalitarianism, individualism, and self-sufficiency. The farmers, craftsmen, and merchants who settled the land carried out an experiment in grass-roots democracy that would have caused considerable misgivings among our skeptical and aristocratic Founding Fathers. Without any authority other than their practical reason and a belief in individual human dignity, they set up self-governing communities which functioned well in the decades before industrial-

Lisel Mueller

2

---

1. My exclusion leaves out several active Chicago poets, including Gwendolyn Brooks, whose sharp-edged portraits of urban, especially black urban, people are among the most valuable poems to have come out of the Midwest.

ism changed the premises on which the society was based. There was no colonial charter, no theocracy to govern public and private conduct; there was no elite of rank and culture nor, in the beginning, of money. Hardship and isolation were accepted as the price for stability and, in many cases, eventual prosperity. For these people, experience was the touchstone of knowledge. As a result, the society was characterized by considerable anti-intellectualism and a distrust of "impractical," abstract thinking. (It is unimaginable that, for example, transcendentalism or the art-for-art's sake movement could have arisen in the Midwest.) This was the region of log-cabin Presidents; there was — and still is — pride in poverty turned success, obscurity turned accomplishment.

The Midwest is known for its political conservatism, yet in the 19th century it allowed communal utopias to flourish in its midst, and it produced in the early 20th century some of America's most fiercely independent minds: political reformers, labor organizers, fighting journalists, and, of course, poets and novelists who, by way of a ruthlessly self-critical literature, attacked the gradual debasement of the pioneer heritage by industrial encroachment, which brought with it ugliness, conformity, corruption, crime, the concentration of wealth and power in the hands of the few, and in general the beginnings of that cheapening of life values which need not be spelled out to the present reader. The writings of the Chicago Renaissance which produced, in the period around World War I, that fortunate concentration of talent and energy which included Masters, Lindsay, Sandburg, Dreiser, and Sherwood Anderson, as well as the start of the little magazine movement through its founders, Harriet Monroe *(Poetry)* and Margaret Anderson *(The Little Review),* are remarkable not for brilliance of style or profundity of ideas, but for their astuteness about people and the impact of social and economic conditions on their relationships and attitudes.

They are remarkable also for a straightforwardness which had not been part of the American literary tradition, and which, for all its realism, did not preclude an optimistic outlook on the future. Change still seemed possible, although the degree of optimism varied. Sandburg, proud of the frontier heritage, saw in the rapidly advancing industrialization a new frontier and a base for further human growth. Masters' "Spoon River," on the other hand, was, like Anderson's "Winesburg, Ohio," faint with praise and heavy with denunciation of small-town life.

I have spent so much time on the Midwestern heritage because I believe the present generation of poets needs to be understood in the light of that heritage. It's no secret that poets have no place in American society, and, in the rugged Midwest especially, the folksy, homespun versifier may be able to feel at home, but the real poet must put up with the status of village idiot. Still, poets have roots no less than other people and, being poets, they are acutely aware of how these roots tug and pull at them. As often as not, it has been the forked desire to break the roots and simultaneously preserve them, which has produced memorable literature in America. It certainly did in the case of Theodore Roethke, the poet from Michigan, who grew up in the greenhouse of his German immigrant father, where he learned to love and rebel and to know and revere nature not as something "wondrous to behold," but as something primal, necessary, life-giving, and therefore beautiful in a sense which had nothing to do with the aesthetic. For Roethke, the knowledge of the interdependence between himself and the most modest forms of nature—root, tuber, worm, snail, and snake—justified and redeemed his own life.

Nature is not usually presented in such minuteness; Roethke was, of course, exceptional in his knowledge of what he called "the minimal." More often, nature appears as landscape. Whatever its shape, it is never a poetic foil, as it often was in New England poetry, nor is it something to be contemplated. It is an existential force, the land which was the benign or disastrous reality of every settler's life. Even now, with nature so diminished, Midwestern poets grant it the respect of close observation. Though symbolic implications may be evident, as they are, for instance, in Jim Harrison's long suites, the images of woods, streams, and orchards are carefully and accurately detailed; there is no compromise with physical reality. Harrison is as conscious of the ecological chain, i.e., the kinship between nature and us, as Roethke was. Not that this is every poet's emphasis. Thomas McGrath's celebrations of the Dakota prairie, with its fields and barns and silos, its heat-shimmering summers and star-hung nights, are above all celebrations of the life soaked in by one human being: himself, the boy who grew up on that prairie. Robert Bly, on the other hand, who continues to write from a farm in Minnesota, finds separate, animate lives in the things of nature, as illustrated here by the closing lines from "Three Kinds of Pleasure":

> It is a pleasure, also, to be driving
> Toward Chicago, near dark,
> And see the lights in the barns,
> The bare trees more dignified than ever,
> Like a fierce man on his deathbed,
> And the ditches along the road half full of a private snow.

Bly's mystical sensibility is not especially typical for Midwestern writing, even its poetry. What I wish to stress here is that he, like the others, keeps coming back to the affinity between man and nature. The ways of perceiving that affinity differ, but the fact that it exists remains constant among these poets. No poet has made us feel it more intimately than William Stafford, whose Kansas poems are bound to endure as testaments of the landscape and its people. To separate "landscape" from "people" in Stafford's poems is just about impossible; both partake of the same life, which is also the life of the poems. Ecology and love: together these make a bond so strong that Stafford's landscape seems to be inhabited by human presences even when no one is named and a poem seems to deal exclusively with nature. Most of the time, however, his poems are specifically concerned with people-and-landscape, or rather, people *in* the landscape. Stafford is haunted by the conjunction; almost every poem speaks of it in some way. In "The Peters Family," people living in a never-ending expanse of fields have been swallowed up by their environment, have become strange:

> You couldn't analyze these people —
> a no-pattern had happened to them:
> their field opened and opened,
> level, and more, then forever,
> never crossed. Their world went everywhere.

The determinism evident in such poems is not limited to Stafford. Whether the environment is industrial or rural, man is what he is, in part at least, because of that environment. People are seen against a background, or within a framework, or through a screen. A black man, who is slowly working himself to death in a St. Louis street, is seen by John Knoepfle through a haze of dust and heat. In a poem by Dave Etter, an old-timer hanging around the county courthouse becomes a fixture of the place, like the spittoon, the cannon, and the racist talk no one thinks of as racist. McGrath's too little-known "pseudo-autobiography," *Letter to an Imaginary Friend* is shot through with portrayals of people, each of whom has his own peculiar relationship to the real world he occupies. One keeps coming back, not to the "human condition" in general, but to individual human lives. Knoepfle has written that he wants his poems to reflect a certain common quality, "something basic and handsome," which he has discovered in persons otherwise quite diverse. And even a poet as unconcerned with region as Mona Van Duyn is solidly Midwestern in this respect. Her poems rejoice in the variety of creatures in the human zoo, with their pleasing and grotesque shapes, their appetites for experience, their lust for every sort of possibility.[2]

This deeply ingrained humanism, this attention and respect accorded the individual person, may well be the special contribution of Midwestern poets to American poetry. It's true that E. A. Robinson in Maine and Robert Frost in Vermont said something similar, but it's also true that both stood essentially apart from the heritage, as well as the current literary trends, in that part of the country. In Mid-America, humanism *was* the tradition, just as free verse, Midwest style, was not a European import, but an introduction of everyday common speech patterns into the province of poetry. The point is that the bias toward naturalness and against formalism was entirely consistent with the egalitarian heritage. Since Masters and Sandburg, Midwestern poets have, of course, been exposed to a great diversity of theoretical and practical influences. Naturalness has gone through assorted sieves. Still, simplicity of diction has remained the rule. Verbal innovation has never made real headway here, and elegance of style has neither been a goal nor a fact. In the old battle between virtuosity and integrity of feeling—battle between paper tigers though it may be—allegiance has never been a problem: Midwestern poets believe that the exposed grain of experience is far more beautiful than any glossy finish.

---

2. It is not my purpose to give a list of Midwestern poets in this paper. In addition to poets referred to, others could have been mentioned. For an extended, though by no means comprehensive anthology of Midwestern poets, see *Heartland*, ed. by Lucien Stryk, Northern Illinois University Press, 1967.

It doesn't follow, however, that the Midwestern experience was necessarily a happy one. Stafford's was; his poems are filled with gratitude for the childhood world to which he owes his life as a poet and a man—a remembered kingdom of love and parental wisdom that he carries inside him like a blessing. But he is very much aware that there is another side to the coin and has written many deeply moving poems about the unfortunate and unhappy people he has known. Dave Etter's poems come through as ambivalent; he creates tension by a mix of affection and bitterness. As a result, his poetry often is ironic in tone, but it can be openly, frankly, painful, like these lines from "Two Dreams of Kansas":

Lisel
Mueller

8

> In a wheatfield
> west of Hays
> the fat thighs of a farm girl
> are clamped around my loins.
> I am dying of loneliness.

But it has been James Wright who has brought forth what must be the saddest poems in the language, poems about unrealized lives in the river towns along the Ohio. (He has also written what must be the most quietly joyful, even ecstatic, poems of our day, but these are poems of revelation, discoveries of himself in the world of natural beings.) Wright's identification is with all those who have been run over by the American Dream; his empathy includes not only the obvious failures, the drifters, prostitutes, and suicides, but also the many whose failure is more subtle, whose despair is submerged. It seems a surprisingly short way from the *Spoon River* of 1915 to a poem like "Autumn Begins in Martins Ferry, Ohio":

> In the Shreve High Football stadium,
> I think of Polacks nursing long beers in Tiltonsville,
> And gray faces of Negroes in the blast furnace at Benwood,
> And the ruptured night watchman of Wheeling Steel,
> Dreaming of heroes.

All the proud fathers are ashamed to go home.
Their women cluck like starved pullets,
Dying for love ...

The difference lies in the hope for alternatives. Masters' gen- eration could conceive of blighted towns and lives as a disease that could be, and well might be, cured. By the time the Sixties came around, there seemed no room left for such opti-
mism. Poets, here and elsewhere, no longer put their hope in
social change; they look to inner, spiritual possibilities for
their salvation. And so we are, after all, a long way from the
decade in which Sherwood Anderson could write about himself and his colleagues: "We were all from the Middle West.
We were all full of hope.... It was the time when something
blossomed in Chicago and the Middle West.... Something
which had been very hard in American life was beginning
to crack and in our group we often spoke of it hopefully."

Something is cracking in American life again; a new consciousness is emerging among the young. But this consciousness is unlike, and by and large antithetical to, the Midwestern tradition; it is precisely that tradition which is cracking.
Poets are aware of what it is that is going beyond hope of
revitalization, where it has not already gone. McGrath and
Stafford are conscious of the fact that they are chroniclers of
history; so is Dave Etter, whose book title *The Last Train to
Prophetstown* is as literally accurate as it is metaphorically
true. Robert Bly calls on us to witness the waste of America
with him:

> Come with me into those things that have felt this
>   despair for so long —
> Those removed Chevrolet wheels that howl with a
>   terrible loneliness,
> Lying on their backs in the cindery dirt, like men
>   drunk, and naked
> Staggering off down a hill at night to drown at last
>   in the pond.

*Lisel
Mueller*
9

And the curly steel shavings, scattered about on
    garage benches,
Sometimes still warm, gritty when we hold them,
Who have given up and blame everything on the
    government,
And those roads in South Dakota that feel around
    in the darkness . . .

Lisel
Mueller

10

The setting is the Midwest, but the physical blight and spiritual desolation are symptomatic of a disease which runs all through America, just as the healing, if indeed we should be lucky enough to produce a really new culture, will run all through America. Poets from the Midwest tend to be specific; they write of the disappearance of the countryside, of tottering farmhouses with broken windows, of highways and shopping centers and parking lots that once were villages, but what they are mourning, of course, is the exhaustion of a distinct culture. Among the middle-aged poets—and this is the generation I have been discussing—nostalgia is strong. But for a poet as young as James Tate, born 1943 in Kansas City, Missouri, it is already too late for nostalgia. He can remember only the breakup; the roots that are still attached to him have lost their purpose, like outworn evolutionary appendages. His poems are full of restlessness, loneliness, a sense of blind alleys; places appear to be formless; human shapes have no substance. The old order is gone: where there was a center, there is a vacuum; where there was stability, there is flux; consumer conformity has taken the place of shared beliefs. Let William Stafford have the last word:

Pioneers, for whom history was walking through dead grass,
and the main things that happened were miles and the times
    of day —
you built that town, and I have let it pass.
Little folded paws, judge me: I came away.

✳

THE ISLAND

For Carl and Irene Krumhardt

Stepping on land,
we feel our skins change
to fit us at last. We are
renewed in some child-god's image,
the past washed away between shores.

We can see clear to the bottom
and, at night, believe in stars.
We might learn enough stillness
to turn into salt-licks for deer
and let our hair grow useful
in a warbler's beak.

Except we know we won't stay
long enough for the spell
to become irreversible, to forget
the unnatural world of death
by filth and gas and the ring of poisons
that hides the Great Bear from us:
the mainland, where the human brain
races in faster and faster circles
of suffering and love
and nothing fits us as well
as do our dreams.

We know we'll flag
a boatload of home-grown saviors,
who speak our fallible language
and fly in the mind only:
our kind, our kind who care.

Lisel
Mueller

11

SMALL POEM
ABOUT THE HOUNDS AND THE HARES

Lisel
Mueller

12

After the kill, there is the feast.
And toward the end, when the dancing subsides
and the young have sneaked off somewhere,
the hounds, drunk on the blood of the hares,
begin to talk of how soft
were their pelts, how graceful their leaps,
how lovely their scared, gentle eyes.

THE AUTOBIOGRAPHY OF MALCOLM X

He had to live his life forward,
but we can run it back;
we can see its form, the peaks,
the curves, plateaus, the jagged angles,
the dislocations, the dead stop.

We can attend his life
at our own pace, go back
to that frame in prison
where he copies the dictionary
by a miserable lightbulb;
privileged, we can run
the mixing of blood and ink
again and again and watch
as he keeps growing and shedding
new skins, as he peels out
always more human, until someone
from a lower order of life
stops his ascent forever.

BEETHOVEN'S NINTH

That verse about a Good Father
living beyond the heavenly tent—
did Beethoven really believe that,
paranoid and deaf?

Lisel
Mueller

13

A hundred and fifty years
after the brotherly dream
we hear it in stereo. We came of age
in the season of Auschwitz. Our brothers
have put on white coats, have gone
to work for the enemy, death.
We have grown middle-aged
on threats of annihilation.

Tulips come open between us.
Under the sun's pressure
whip-scars as old as Beethoven's music
erupt on the bodies of armed black men.
Outside our door the aspen
—beautiful innocent—bursts
into thousands of small lives.
I hear the voices of singers
from a supposedly foreign land
strain with the same incredible joy
that strains your face, my unbeliever,
my gentle scoffer, not scoffing now.

Spring 1969

MESSAGES

*Lisel
Mueller*

Outside the window, messages pile up,
congratulations, valentines,
spring bouquets with assurances
about the dancing feet of the dead
which we swore we had had enough of.

A day of glorious weather
is all it takes to corrupt us;
we betray the grief we wanted to keep
like a broken watch, we decide
the anger we thought was integrity
was, after all, only anger.

We fill the mouths of the speechless
with tongues and delight in their news,
forgetting who put it there;
we receive like the woman whose teeth
contain too much metal, who eavesdrops
on the radio signals of fishermen
and lies awake on her coil of springs
listening to music from God knows where.

After the shootings, we understood
the stiffened air, the reversal
of tulips from silk to paper
and knew why the ground resisted
the small weaponry of our heels.

We breathe all things into speech;
we listen, we respond.
The doorknob insists that we turn it,
an unopened letter demands its rights.

Dogs talk to us with their bodies
and accept our answer in words.
Holes ask for rain; the stunted corpse of an elm
is revealed as a sign. We keep breaking
the code of the dead, we reply.

THE LEVITATION

Now in the space between sleep and waking,
  the heart expands in its rubber skin,
eyes and lips have fallen away,
and the long bones lie unarmed
in shallow trenches of flesh.

Whatever exists is floating:
words without weight, bodies without resistance,
feelings wavy as trailing scarves
move through the gently dissolving center
between heaven and earth where we live,
briefly, in a mild light.

THE PICTURE FROM CHINA

In the picture from China
the children's naked bellies
endure their unwilled lives
like open flowers.

God dips among them,
a huge black bee,
carrying death
from cup to cup.

ON FINDING A BIRD'S BONES IN THE WOODS

Even Einstein, gazing
at the slender ribs of the world,
examining and praising
the cool and tranquil core
under the boil and burning
of faith and metaphor—
even he, unlearning
the bag and baggage of notion,
must have kept some shred
in which to clothe that shape,
as we, who cannot escape
imagination, swaddle
this tiny world of bone
in all that we have known
of sound and motion.

HIGHWAY 2, ILLINOIS

Look at this country,
those shapeless multiple greens,
haphazard, inhumanly lost:
but for the barns,
the colorful mothers,
settling them all like wayward children
around their sturdy skirts,

where would all that loneliness go?

A FAREWELL, A WELCOME

After the lunar landings

Goodbye pale cold inconstant
tease, you never existed
therefore we had to invent you

Lisel
Mueller

17

        Goodbye crooked little man
        huntress who sleeps alone
        dear pastor, shepherd of stars
        who tucked us in   Goodbye

Good riddance phony prop
con man moon
who tap-danced with June
to the tender surrender
of love from above

Goodbye decanter of magic liquids
fortune teller *par excellence*
seducer   incubus   medicine man
exile's sanity   love's sealed lips
womb that nourished the monstrous child
and the sweet ripe grain   Goodbye

        We trade you in as we traded
        the evil eye for the virus
        the rosy seat of affections
        for the indispensable pump
we say goodbye as we said goodbye
to angels in nightgowns   to Grandfather God

Goodbye forever Edam and Gorgonzola
cantaloupe in the sky
night-watchman, one-eyed loner
    wolves nevertheless

are programmed to howl   Goodbye
forbidden lover goodbye
sleepwalkers will wander
with outstretched arms for no reason
while you continue routinely
to husband the sea, prevail
in the fix of infant strabismus

Goodbye ripe ovum   women will spill their blood
in spite of you now   lunatics wave goodbye
accepting despair by another name
Welcome new world to the brave old words
peace   hope   justice
truth everlasting   welcome
ash-colored playground of children
happy in airy bags
never to touch is never to miss it

Scarface hello   we've got you covered
welcome untouchable   outlaw
with an alias in every country
salvos and roses   you are home
our footprints stamp you mortal

*

A SELECTIVE BIBLIOGRAPHY

1. Collections of poetry

Dependencies, University of North Carolina Press, Chapel Hill, 1965.
Life of a Queen, Juniper Press, 1970.

2. Anthologies containing individual poems

Best Poems of 1968, Pacific Books, 1960.
Best Poems of 1960, Pacific Books, 1962.
The Contemporary American Poets, edited by Mark Strand, New American Library, 1969.
Heartland, edited by Lucien Stryk, Northern Illinois University Press, 1967.
I Love You All Day, it is that simple, edited by Philip Dacey and Gerald M. Knoll, Abbey Press, 1970.
Inside Outer Space, edited by Robert Vas Dias, Doubleday, 1970.
The New Yorker Book of Poems, edited by members of *The New Yorker,* Viking, 1969.
To Play Man Number One, edited by Sara Hannum and John Terry Chase, Atheneum, 1969.

3. Magazines containing poems not included in the author's two collections.

Cafe Solo. #3.
Chicago Tribune Magazine, January 21, 1968, December 15, 1968.
Intermission, September 1966.
The New Yorker, November 4, 1967.
Poetry, July 1967, November 1969, February 1970.
Shenandoah, Winter 1968, Spring 1970.

4. Critical articles

"Digging the Universe," *Poetry*, January 1968. (On Gary Snyder.)

"Five Poets," *Shenandoah*, Spring 1968.

"Four Poets," *Poetry*, October 1966.

"German Chronicle," *Poetry*, February 1968.

"Poetry Chronicle," *Poetry*, January 1966.

"A Poetic Pilgrimage: The Life Work of Roethke," *Panorama*, The Chicago *Daily News*, July 23, 1966.

"The Sun the Other Way Around," *Poetry*, August 1966. (On Elizabeth Bishop.)

"To Love the Enigma," *Poetry*, February 1961. (On Rilke.)

(Other reviews of poetry have appeared, at irregular intervals, in *Panorama*, The Chicago *Daily News*, since 1965.)

5. Miscellaneous work

"The Salzburg Great Theater of the World," by Hugo von Hofmannsthal, translated by the author in collaboration with John Reich. A performing version of the play, given at Goodman Theatre, Chicago, in 1968. (Not in print.)

John Knoepfle

*

POETRY IN THE FIFTIES:
A PERSONAL VIEW

*John
Knoepfle*
23

SOMETIMES A WRITER is deep in his own ego because he is guarding a secret. What he has to say, or is going to say, is not clearly understood in his own mind. At this stage of his development he is vulnerable and dependent on the encouragement of a few friends. Otherwise he will not be able to continue with his work. There are too many good reasons for quitting. He is rejected so much that, looking back, looking at the poems that were not accepted for such good reasons, he wonders if he had anything going for him but his own incredible arrogance. I don't know. Maybe arrogance is not the right word. Perhaps what he has to carry him along is a sense of the importance of time, slow time, time enough to let that secret open up in him and come by degrees into his work. He goes his way, writing his poems, and if he is lucky, the poems tell his secret.

On the same count, to go back, to be articulate about his beginnings, is painful. He has to work at it, but in the process he discovers so many things he had forgotten that it is as if he had to take the time to confront shadows and ask for a blessing. If not, what he produces is his own image in his remembrance. I would like to avoid this, but frankly, do not know how it is possible. I am not very good at asking for blessings, and to tell the truth, have never enjoyed talking about my past. I guess it is because I have become happier as I have grown older.

Well, when the wind rises all the leaves blow in the same general direction, although they appear to be tossing in every direction. I see now that the poets of the fifties were turning to experiences which had been abandoned, which were not then in the mainstream of the nation's thought, dreams that had been burned and gutted, junked like the furnace in W.S. Merwin's poem. We wanted to return to these, impelled by some guilt, I suppose, and by some hope. We identified with busted lives, people who had not made it, people who were at fault, people who were busted even though they were not at fault. Recalling this, it seems beyond belief, but we were buffeting the strange complacency of the atomic years after world war two. It is easy to forget that in those days a successful man paid homage to his individuality by cultivating a harmless eccentricity. And then the poets began to establish their bad castles, and even poets who were friendly were suspected of evil intentions:

> Where he gets his spirits
> It's a mystery. But the stuff keeps him musical:
> Hammer-and-anvilling with poker and bottle
> to his jugged bellowing.

Empty furnaces were being stoked across the country, and people were beginning to hear unexpected noises inside of them.

It seems to have mattered a great deal at that time where we started from; no one could have imagined Lowell and Ginsberg and Bly in Merwin's furnace, but they were all there. They were like people who decided to go fishing, not knowing what they would catch, and who cast their nets out on the water and caught amazing things, including themselves. They were poets, post war, post nuclear, who could no longer live in romantic isolation or in the lonely classical dominance of the art-making ego.

Robert Bly heard in the snowy fields of Minnesota:

Cries, half-muffled, from beneath the earth, the living awakened at last like the dead.

And if this condition had been altered radically, so that the dead were made to awaken at last like the living, these cries could have been heard among the people Galway Kinnell brooded over in the kingdom that was on Avenue C:

> This God-forsaken Avenue bearing the initial of Christ
> Through the haste and carelessness of the ages,
> Where the drowned suffer a C-change,
> And remain the common poor.

For James Wright the furnace became a crucible:

> Miners paused here on the way up to Alaska.
> Angry, they spaded their broken women's bodies
> Into ditches of crab grass.
> I lie down between tombstones.

In "Memories of West Street and Lepke," Lowell asserted the existence of a society that the fifties would rather have denied, a society of thugs, delinquents, murderers, conscientious objectors, pimps and Jehovah's Witnesses, a society of dangerous men, each one isolated in his own particular version of the American dream. They were figures that were scarcely visible in the fifties, but today they are very much alive on the streets and in the news.

There was a preoccupation in these years with death, or perhaps not so much with death as with the dead. Possibly this was another aspect of that divided vision which so much has been made of since the beginning of the century, or possibly it was caused by the horrifying events of the second world war with its aftermath of cities and nations of dead created at a stroke, or it may have been the religious quickening that took place in the late forties which tended to establish a communion between the living and the dead.

Allen Ginsberg, for example, wrote a poem of praise and lament that records the life and death of his mother, Naomi, and recaptures the Buchenwalds and flowering loves of a middle class, idealistic, Jewish, broken existence. It is documented with an almost masochistic rigor; yet the poem, along with whatever else it is, is a narrative of an escape, a way out of a prison and into a country. The poem ends with a crow cawing praises to the Lord over the gravestones of Long Island, a terrible mixed up praise and scream. With "Kaddish" Allen Ginsberg broke down WASP walls: he demanded the entrance of Naomi Ginsberg into the mainstream of American consciousness, and he got it.

Gary Snyder's *Myths and Texts* is an exhilarating book. It is surprising to recollect, suddenly, in the midst of so much vitality how much of this experience is owed to the presence of the dead. A passage in the book reawakens an old revolution, as so much that is in "Kaddish" recalls the lost Communist movement in New York; but this time

'Forming the New Society
Within the shell of the Old'
The motto in the Wobbly Hall
Some old Finns and Swedes playing cards
Fourth and Yesler in Seattle.
O you modest, retiring, virtuous young ladies
    pick the watercress, pluck the yarrow
'Kwan kwan' goes the crane in the field,
    I'll meet you tomorrow;
A million workers dressed in black and buried,
We make love in leafy shade.

Here is the inevitable juxtaposition of disparate experiences, almost a point of departure for poets of the fifties, immersed as they were in unresolved relationships. In *Myths and Texts,* however, the leap from one thing to another has some of the pleasure and some of the illusion of infinite visibility that is characteristic of high mountain country, but there is more to it than this: the dead speak to the living here. The lovers are not totally separated from the buried workers, nor are the old men cut off from the strange call of the crane.

There is a sense of possibilities of new relationships, of a new society gathering itself together within the shell of the old.

The unpretentious poems of William Stafford chronicle the journey of a man through space and time. He sets a high value on the places he has come from and come to and he has a tender regard for those people who have lived and died in them without a spokesman. His poems, it seems to me, represent a sustained attempt to confer some small immortality upon the companions and friends of his childhood, a determination that no one will be lost:

> In other towns, calling my name,
> home people hail me, dazed;
> those moments we hold,
> reciting in the evening,
>
> Reciting about you, receding
> through the huddle of any new town.
> Can we rescue the light
> that happened, and keeps on happening,
>   around us?

He is as aware as Gary Snyder that once a man sets foot in a country, that land lives in him and by him, and that its meaning must be expressed through him, or not at all. He clings fiercely to this awareness:

> They call it regional, this relevance —
> the deepest place we have: in this pool forms
> the model of our land, a lonely one,
> responsive to the wind. Everything we own
> has brought us here: from here we speak.
>
> The sun stalks among these peaks to sight
> the lake down aisles, long like a gun;
> a ferryboat, lost by a century, toots
> for trappers, the pelt of the mountains
> rinsed in the sun and that sound.

But he lives in his own time, too, so much so that a tragic, local event, a windstorm in the midwest, something remembered from his past, becomes the expression of the state of mind of a multitude of people following the days of world war two:

> We weren't left religion exactly (the church
> was ecumenical bricks), but a certain tall element:
> a pulse beat still in the stilled rock
> and in the buried sound along the buried mouth of the creek.

These poets are surely a mixed group. And considering their backgrounds, they would seem unlikely to be writing the kind of poems touched on above. They are graduates of Harvard, Princeton, Columbia, Kenyon, and super-graduates of Iowa and Washington, and Gary Snyder has four years of work in descriptive linguistics to his credit. But they represent, each in his own way, the strong desire among the poets of the fifties to redeem the lost history of America's immediate past, that story of the movement of peoples within the nation that was suppressed in the final volumes of all the local histories when the subscriptions were sold and the pages were filled with biographies of only the most important citizens, the leaders in the community, prominent churchmen, presidents of banks, corporations, and country clubs, or families that counted.

In a sense, this turning to a lost history in the fifties is something that could have been predicted. Reading F. O. Matthiessen whose *American Renaissance* was published in 1941, I can see much of what this history meant to us, spelled out with a quiet passion in his interpretation of nineteenth century American literature. Other works which foreshadowed the particular drift of the fifties were *In the American Grain* and *Studies in Classic American Literature*, both out in the twenties. But having said this, I have to say that I find it a deep mystery that these poets should have responded in the way that they did, or that I myself should identify with them. Maybe there was a streak of old populist in all of us.

I cannot explain how this man or that came to his position, but I can, with some labor and much self-doubt, speak for myself. I have to be honest. I did read the moderns. I read all of Frost, and learned much from his work, and to this day have a certain sympathy for his problems. He could do anything that any other poet of his time could do, but he was not as exciting to critics as Pound and Eliot, and so had to go his own way, and I imagine that in his middle years it must have been a lonely one. Even so, I read for something that was not in Frost or in Robinson either. At that time I did not know what this was, but I know now. It was a feeling for the folk that neither ignores nor disdains the deep religious sensitivity of the folk. And I have learned this from hearing the music of Charles Ives that speaks for this sensitivity with a fullness that I have not seen expressed anywhere, except perhaps in the lines of Stafford.

I read T. S. Eliot, and I suppose drank all the water I could hold at his spring. He was an important social force, and made it possible to think that Catholicism might be relevant to the nuclear age because Anglicanism was. Beyond this, Eliot was foreign to me. The rich people in "Waste Land" and in "Prufrock" were not like the rich people I knew in Cincinnati. Eliot's rich were too removed from the sources of their money. The poor people he described were again unlike the poor I knew. My second cousins lived on the Lower East Side. I can remember the family portraits on the walls of their apartment, men, women, and children in their best clothes, looking very formal, very dignified. These people had not been rich, and some of them had been very poor, but they were not like the crowds that Eliot wrote about or the individual sketches that he made in his poems. A few years ago I would have said that he was a snob. Today I assume that he accepted a seventeenth century dramatic convention to distinguish the personalities in his works. It is a convention that I cannot apply in this country. I do not think that being poor in America has anything to do with carnality, sensuality, or the loss of intellect. And so my guard was up with Eliot, also.

I read all of Yeats, and must confess that he touched me where I was most defenseless. I even had by heart some of his poems of bewildered love, they were so in tune with my bachelor experiences. I liked him also because he was Irish, and at that time I identified chauvinistically with my maternal grandparents. But since then I have been put off by his attentiveness to decorum and ceremony because I have learned that these when ritualized serve to perpetuate injustice.

It must be evident how subjective and personal my reactions to other poets were. I will have to defend myself by saying again that we make poems out of our secrets, and that we have to protect these from the consuming greatness of others.

I was a parochial school kid who had gone through world war two and returned to continue my life as a member of the largest subculture in the United States and the least represented in this nation's literature. The modern Catholic literary tradition that I inherited was European. It included Mauriac, Bloy, Peguy, Bernanos, Undset, Martindale, Greene, C. S. Lewis, Waugh, and D'Arcy. I read these authors so fiercely that many of my Catholic friends thought I was becoming a communist. I was not, however, able to write poems from this tradition. Another writer who comes to mind in this context is Gerard Manley Hopkins. His work and his conception of "inscape" heavily influenced a number of contemporaries of mine who went off in other directions, other poets of the fifties, but that is material for another essay.

Very likely I could not have developed as I did without the presence of Thomas Merton. I see this as I try to assess the meaning of the fifties for me, but I did not realize it at the time. Merton came from a cosmopolitan background. He had been in on the jazz scene in New York, had written a thesis on Blake, had observed ancient Roman and Renaissance art in Europe, and had come somewhat to his conversion by reading James Joyce, a far in thing in the late forties. He had done all this, and yet there he was a monk in a medieval monastery near Bardstown, Kentucky, speaking of "my Israel in the Ohio valley" and in "Elias" converting Blake's chariot of fire into an old trailer:

> faster and faster it stands still,
> faster and faster it stays where it has always been,

giving me an opening into my own region.

It is difficult to describe exactly what this opening involved. Certainly part of it was Merton's straightforward incorporation of Kentucky, past, present, and future, landscape and people, into the dogmatic and timeless verities of preconsular Catholicism. Only an outsider could have done that with no foot-shuffling apologetics. For me this helped to reconcile a personal faith with the kind of lost American history that was very real to me. I puzzled how to make this reconciliation in the first long river poem that I wrote, how to ransom for grace the industrial river I saw below me from Eden Park in Cincinnati. The poem was rejected by an editor who was glad to know that someone was still writing in the grand old tradition of Carl Sandburg. I struggled with this problem again, and I hope somehow resolved it, in a later poem, "Church of Rose of Lima, Cincinnati." The last line of the poem provided the title to *Rivers into Islands*.

However, the deepest effect that Merton had on me was of a more subtle and less explicit nature. It was his sense of work as liturgy and liturgy as public work, daily work which had the potency "to build new societies within the shell of the old," that released my baroque mind. When I wrote about the river or of men laboring on the river or described the violence of the Harpe brothers or spoke of what I had seen in East St. Louis or drew materials from the past of my own family, I felt that I was writing in my own tradition, and, finally, that this writing was in some way relevant to the present.

A more intimate influence was the presence of another working poet who was also a friend. John Logan grew up in Red Oak, Iowa. A graduate of Coe College with a number of scholarships to medical schools, he ultimately chose to take his chances as a poet. In the early fifties he became a Catholic, taking, almost incongruously, Mother Cabrini as his patroness. She was an Italian immigrant and naturalized citizen who ministered to the poor, and the first saint from the United States to be formally canonized. I met him shortly after he published his first book, *A Cycle for Mother Cabrini* which was well received in both the Catholic and the secular press. He was the first established writer to take a serious look at my work, and did so at a moment when I was ready to give up poetry. He bolstered my flagging intuition that the river materials were valuable and encouraged me to continue in the narrative vein at a time when few other poets were interested in this mode.

But in the middle fifties there were other influences, and these were to absorb my interest almost to the exclusion of Merton, so that only one poem in *Rivers into Islands* consciously reflects his work. This poem is "June Night on the River" and the monks referred to in it, though not necessarily spelled out as such in the poem, were from the abandoned monastery on Cahokia Mound, the early Trappist settlement on the east side of the river opposite St. Louis. The monks of Athos who are referred to were derived from an article on Eastern Rite monasticism which Merton wrote for *Jubilee*. That article was the last work of Merton's that I read closely, and at the time it was published I was already deep into the novels of Dostoevski and the poems of Vallejo and Garcia-Lorca. I wondered at their ability to represent whole societies in their work, to allow peoples apart from themselves to come through what they wrote. I was puzzling, too, the line from the Navaho song which was sung by the women and children for their men when that nation was in captivity: "Everywhere I go, joy surrounds me." It seemed to me that these artists possessed some depth of understanding that I could not locate in my own land, and I wanted to search for this depth in us. I believe that many others were moving in this direction at this time, so that I came to know the work of Bly, Wright, Louis Simpson, Merwin, and others with a happy sense of recognition.

These poets, as it turned out, were also hearing voices from the outside. They were also being influenced by work and ideas from elsewhere: Robert Bly and James Wright by the rediscovery of European, Hispanic and Latin American, and Asian poetry; Gary Snyder by the discipline of Zen and the myths of North American Indians; Ginsberg by Eastern mysticism, enabling him to formulate his own particular hip vision. It seems that this vast migration of Americans into their own selves and into their own country that some of us were writing about was an international phenomenon. It could not have come about unless voices from other cultures had ratified our secrets and taught us to be ourselves, voices that were not heard in the Classical and Renaissance traditions of Western Europe.

Shortly after Merton's death in Bangkok in 1968, I read Eldridge Cleaver's account in *Soul on Ice* of his own complicated responses during the late fifties and early sixties to the work of this Trappist monk. It was finally Merton's "no" to the society that had wasted Harlem which Cleaver accepted and incorporated into his own activities as a Black Muslim and revolutionary. That the context of our experience was different, the history of the last few years has shown bitterly. But something about the encounter was the same, the moment of ratification of a personal identity from an unexpected source. It is almost a classic experience: Malcolm X goes to Elijah Muhammad and to Africa; Dr. King turns in his travail to Mahatma Gandhi.

Looking back now, it seems that many aspects of the movement that was going on in black America during the fifties and early sixties was a far reaching popular manifestation of some concerns I have tried to speak about, from an entirely different background, in this essay: the need to bring the past into the present, the need to end impotencies of isolation in the frozen violence of that post war society, to identify oneself and to make this identification in a way that was, in one sense or another, religious. This is how it appears to me as I remember these concerns and trace them into the polarized but unhidden America of the sixties and seventies.

young girls song

my father is looking at me
and I am shamefaced
I don't know why he is smiling
my mother is singing in the kitchen
my brothers are winking
they are making silly faces

*John
Knoepfle*
35

I hope he does not see me
watching through the blinds
he has come walking by my house
fourteen times this morning
he seems to be staring
at red birds in the cottonwood tree

I must pretend I am alone
my joy is three white roses
hidden in a blue bush
my joy throws red birds in the air
and I am full and overflowing
like the singing of my mother

from *Songs for Gail Guidry's Guitar*. New York: New Rivers Press, 1969.
First published in "Today."

october

John
Knoepfle

36

we halloween
the real dead with candy
for the sake of the children
the dead who cannot rise
blasted and pumpkined
from the jackolantern smiles
of old folks

groundfog
has closed the airport
at kirksville
fog in the meadows
patches of fog on the highway
all the way north

beeswax ignites
the candied apple
skulls of the living
who hide in a dozen masks
in the corners of their houses
the souls of their faces
bleeding

rain pours in sheets
across the town square
a blonde
witch in her costume
a small unhappy girl
looks up into the rain

from *The Intricate land*, first printed in "Aardwolf."

in middle kentucky

bluegrass boone burley leaf
lovely country
and poor mens houses
falling down on their heads

John
Knoepfle

37

how you gonna run with these
fine horses jeremiah

poor man couldn't trade
his bourbon gut
for a cedar post

boone didn't want to come back

now they are all boones
black and white boones
running like hell

from *The Intricate Land.*

children

outside my window
I hear my children
bickering in the yard
sparrows of the race
contentious who cannot provide
innocent because
they have no foresight
owls of my own darkness

from *The Intricate Land,* first printed in "The St. Louis Free Press."

after gray days

John
Knoepfle
38

nobody knows
what to do

you take pills
get the word from television
eat right food
you wander around an afternoon

when its raining
your blood wants you to whittle
but that isn't done now

then someone comes up on the porch
with his hair beading water
and rain dripping off his nose

he says that the chinese
think of america
as that far country
of a thousand flowers

you smile at him suddenly
you think if you could only
release maybe fifty million balloons
over asia saying good luck to you china
from the land of a thousand flowers
some golden years
might pour down time

you peer through store windows
watching the shoplifters
you think why are we all
thieves in our bandages

and the snakes in the rocks hissing
come crush our heads
flay us hang our long skins
on the screen doors of your houses

from *The Intricate Land,* first printed in "Sou'wester"; also in *After Gray Days and Other Poems.* Prairie Village, Kansas: Crabgrass Press, 1969.

for lucien vic norman
john frieda rocco frank linda
walter ann kelly jett ted
elaine al ed leola and joe

I write
of our days
of springs
of caves
of places
we have come from
of a quarter turn
another season
of us in our names
with our chance
at joy
of waters
under earth
of flowers
in the mountains
melting
through snow

from *The Intricate Land.*

battlefield at lexington

I stroll the crown of the hill
with my turbulent sons
the thick grass
softens embankments and the trenches
we are on the edge of the bluffs
below a far reach for the eye
the missouri wanders in its flood plain

on this height there is only silence
the unbelievable silence
of fields history has done with
an everlasting payment
for the cannonades of death
that jarred three days here

the river in the sun is a fishhook
that would catch the world

and christopher cries out
you are walking on dead people
there are dead people buried here
his shrill voice darts in the afternoon
like a swallow

*John
Knoepfle*

40

poem for a child

two pieces of bread
on a blue plate
elderberry jelly
purple in a jar
a tablecloth
printed with deep red roses
elderberry bread and red roses
what will you trade for these

John
Knoepfle

41

the wound has its own voice

the language spoken by the wound
how does it sound
has it authority
a record of achievement
that the leader of a nation
will listen to
or is it an ornamental accessory
to a sharp pain
a mirror for a mind
gone underground
a ribbon on a hat the bright
colors of birds buffeting the wind
or is it something so basic
that only the man
concealed in the wound
can imitate its cry

owning myself

John
Knoepfle

42

I have no official capacity
you don't know me
I do not protrude beyond
my surrounding part
there are no designs on my surface
formal beginnings or endings
I am a member of a royal family
I emit visible light
I become incandescent
I can produce magical effects
I am a small island
eroding little by little
I can be provoked into action
you cannot exchange money for my services
I slope toward death
while listening with sympathy
bending my head
to the anguish of others
I work hard to elude public notice
I am a sharp instrument
blunted from too much probing.

staring at the wall

his clenched fist
should have held grain
anger is eternal
we have to be afraid

the atmosphere was luminous
with our own cells

walking awkwardly
proceeding haltingly
being in pawn
being held in jail
being in debt
deceived
by formulas of conjurers
we wanted something more
than the appearance of an idea

they said of us
we were bewildered
we thought something good of us
and it was not so

John
Knoepfle

43

not in the public directory

clown clown clown clown
spicy fragrance
formed into clots
an immediate vote
on the question of humanity
fed on by moths
finished off in rags
a hole in the belly
staunched with rags
a small private chamber
for meditation on spindle legs
a narrow escape
hindered by wooden-soled shoes

sometimes I feel good about things

*John
Knoepfle*

44

calm easy going
making love in a mist
feeling love
exhibiting love
having low intensity
but not clumsy
rather a rhombus than a square
providing an escape for smoke
making an offer
falling in a meadow
gladly like snow

BIBLIOGRAPHY

"Among First Books," *Chicago Daily News,* 6 October 1965.

Benoit, Raymond, "The Reflective Art of John Knoepfle," *The Minnesota Review,* VIII, No. 3 (1968), 254-257.

Burke, John Gordon, "An Interview with John Knoepfle," *Missouri Library Association Quarterly,* (March, 1969), 43-48.

Candelaria, Frederick, "Tapes, Inlets, Islands, Hands, and Fingers," *Northwest Review,* (Spring-Summer, 1969). 71-75.

Cuscaden, Robert R., "The Poetry of John Knoepfle," *Steppenwolf,* (1966).

Goldman, Lloyd, "Masks of Self-deception," *The Minnesota Review,* VIII, No. 3 (1968), 258-262.

Ignatow, David, "Including Some Lines of Candid Beauty," *New York Times Book Review,* 14 November 1965.

Knoll, John, "Crisis in the Voice: An Interview with John Knoepfle," *Sou'wester,* (Fall, 1966), 50-57.

Lyle, Katie Fletcher, "Wanted, the Profession Plus the Gift," *The Roanoke Times,* 8 May 1966.

Malanga, Gerard, "Three Firsts," *Poetry: A Magazine of Verse,* (May, 1966), 130-133.

Martz, Louis L., "Recent Poetry: Looking for a Home," *The Yale Review,* (Spring, 1966), 458-469.

Murphy, Rosalie, *Contemporary Poets of The English Language.* Chicago, London: St. James Press, 1970, p. 612.

Scott, James F., "The Metropolitan Sensibility: Notes on Four Poets of St. Louis," *Cross Currents,* (Fall, 1965), 487-491.

- - - - - *Thought,* (Spring, 1966), 140-142.

Smith, Ray, "Brevity is the Soul of Poetry," *Globe-Gazette,* (Mason City, Iowa), 18 September 1965.

- - - - - *Library Journal,* (August, 1965), 3295-3296.

Stryk, Lucien, "New Verse," *Chicago Review No. 59,* 107-110.

Woo, William F., "Old Steamboat Days Recaptured on Tape," *St. Louis Post Dispatch,* 16 May 1966.

✳

Dave Etter

THE ROAD TO THE POEM

An Autobiographical Fragment

Dave Etter

Every man and in particular every American is anxious to tell you his life history. He wants to explain himself.
—Sherwood Anderson

THE POEM WAS ALWAYS THERE, ready to be seized and nailed to the door, to be wooed, possessed, and chained to the bed. But for 25 years, I was not there, not where the poem was, breathing seductively on its printed page. No, I was always on the go, tirelessly moving through the lush, overgrown wilderness of a green and groping adolescence and an awkward and unsettled young manhood. My goal in those early years was a simple one: I wanted to consume as much of the sweet, heady, sun-warmed wine of a life that presented itself to me in so many startling shapes and dazzling colors.

I grew up in a small California town filled with orange trees and vacant lots. Grammar school was a pleasant experience. Home life was solid and middle class. I was normal and obedient. My school work came easily and I was mildly interested in just about everything. In the Sixth Grade, the teacher asked us to memorize a few short poems, selections from Longfellow, Whittier, and other 19th-century American poets. I did what she asked and that was that, another small hurdle cleared on the way to promotion to the Seventh Grade.

My next sideswipe with the poem came about when the local weekly newspaper offered 15 uncancelled foreign stamps to any kid who could write a 12-line poem without using the letter E. I collected stamps, I wanted those stamps, and I was going to get those stamps. So, with considerable help from my Aunt Roberta, I wrote the 12 lines, using nary an E, and obtained what I so very much desired. The whole thing was a gimmick, of course, and was certainly not designed with the idea of getting anyone interested in the poem. It didn't.

In high school, I became a serious student — of girls and baseball. Classes were to be endured, nothing more. In my senior year I made All-League at third base and never missed a school dance. Any possible chance of discovering the poem during those happy-go-lucky years was undoubtedly killed by the stuff we were forced to read: Matthew Arnold's "Sohrab and Rustum," for instance. What nonsense, I thought, about as attractive and useful as a wet towel in the locker room.

As a student firmly entrenched in the academic second division, I looked forward to college about as much as a man with bad teeth looks forward to a trip to the dentist. After two years at the nearest junior college, where I majored in Clock-Watching and minored in Window-Gazing, I decided that I had had it with formal education. Any ideas that I cherished about playing professional baseball went down the drain when I severely wrecked my ankle during a championship game in my second year. So what was I going to do now? While I was pondering my fate, the local draft board began sending me nasty letters. I quickly came to the decision that continuing with college was not such a bad idea after all.

Safely enrolled at the University of Iowa, I finally ran into some pretty good teachers and began to get interested in American history and American literature. I even started writing a few short stories in my room at night. Could writing be what I was looking for? I was hopeful, but unconvinced that anything would come of it. I finally graduated in June 1953, blissfully unaware that the famous Iowa Writers' Workshop had that year served up the likes of Robert Lowell and Karl Shapiro on their picnic table. But then I was far too busy learning about the Schleswig-Holstein question, and the Byzantine period in Russian architecture, and trying to get through a stiff course in Business Arithmetic covering some snappy problems in long division, to rub shoulders with the horn-rimmed crowd.

At the end of the summer, the draft board ran out of patience and I ran out of excuses. The Korean shoot-out was over by then and my friends and neighbors thought it would be safe (for the country, that is) for me to do a two-year stretch at Fort Ord, California. Broke, unhappy, and weakened by the scholarly life, I went quietly. Soon after being introduced to the fashionable rising time of 4 a.m. and learning the fine points of taking a man's head off with a bayonet, I came down with a bad case of pneumonia. In the hospital I slept for a week before I felt strong enough to slip into my paper slippers and make the short trip to the library. The first book I put my hands on was a new volume of Robert Frost's poems, *The Road Not Taken,* edited by Louis Untermeyer, with handsome line drawings of rural New England by John O'Hara Cosgrave II. I checked the book out and returned immediately to my cot. Whether it was the poems or the pictures that excited me first, I cannot recall. I only know that the book took me to an attractive, peaceful setting far from the regimented life of an army base, and that was reward enough. I spent the remainder of my convalescence with Frost and Cosgrave and then was invited to try basic training again. I joined my new company with a fresh outlook on life, however, because I had decided something important: I was going to be a poet.

Upon finishing basic training and clerk-typist school, I was assigned a desk job and kept regular office hours. I now had much more free time and began reading every volume of poetry in the library, from Conrad Aiken to William Carlos Williams. I formed quick opinions in those days. I preferred (and still do) the poets who write on the American scene using the American idiom: Frost, Carl Sandburg, Vachel Lindsay, Edgar Lee Masters, Archibald MacLeish, Stephen Vincent Benet, and, of course, Walt Whitman. But I also became attached to several foreign poets, especially Dylan Thomas, Federico Garcia Lorca, Boris Pasternak, and the French surrealists. I did not take to T. S. Eliot, Ezra Pound, Wallace Stevens, John Crowe Ransom, Allen Tate, and all those younger academic poets attempting to follow in their footsteps. Then, suddenly, it was time to try to write a poem of my own. I put down a few lines, later added a few more, revised the whole thing a couple of times, and then, with a blowing of trumpets, a very ugly duckling of a poem was born. It was just barely good enough to convince myself that I had a pinch of talent and should, therefore, let fly with another one.

The word was soon out that PFC Etter was writing poetry. But that was okay. Almost everyone in the barracks was doing something connected with the arts. We had actors from Idaho, novelists from Oregon, singers from Kansas, and nearby, a WAC who could yodel loud enough to rattle the latrine windows. If PFC Etter wanted to spend his free time writing poetry, well, fine and dandy. In fact, a couple of my drinking companions came along with me while I tried to get a glimpse of the area's only big-time poet, Robinson Jeffers. I did manage to see part of his house, but the old recluse remained out of sight and was no doubt brooding over a new poem based on his beloved Greek myths.

Just as I was getting used to the army coffee, the heavy fogs from the Pacific Ocean, and the character-building walks on early-morning guard duty, I was discharged. I decided to travel, to any place, in any direction. A friend of mine suggested an automobile trip to New York City. He said we would take our time getting there and would spend about three weeks in the south, with a couple of days and nights in New Orleans. I agreed and we took off in my car, saving money along the way by sleeping in the local YMCA, when we couldn't locate a friend or relative who would put us up. After dropping my friend in Manhattan, I headed west, ending up in Cedar Rapids, Iowa, where I applied for unemployment benefits. I landed a job the second week I was there, keeping records for an electronics firm. I worked in a basement and had to call upstairs every noon to find out what the weather was like before I dressed for a blue-plate special at the drugstore. In my free time I roamed the brick streets of the downtown section, taking notes and forming impressions. Back in my rented room, I wrote poems, throwing most of my efforts in the scrap basket. Paul Engle accepted me for the Iowa Poetry Workshop, but the thought of sitting in a classroom again so nauseated me that I forgot the whole thing.

Six months in Cedar Rapids proved sufficient. I was restless to move on. An army buddy wrote saying that life in Worcester, Massachusetts, was not bad. I got out there as fast as I could and again accepted menial employment, this time working for a tiny industrial company for $40 per week. On weekends, I climbed into my faithful Chevy and toured Vermont, New Hampshire, Massachusetts, and Connecticut; and I even found time for a trip to Toronto, Canada. I wrote poems on long pieces of cardboard (why, I don't know), obtained from the laundry that did my shirts. And all this time my brain was in a constant state of turmoil, and I had trouble sleeping. This was my Thomas Wolfe period. I was excited beyond belief by all the smells, sights, and sounds of America. I was determined to attain all knowledge and to know all experience. And I went about it frantically. There were too many books to read, too many places to see, too many people to know. I felt that my job hemmed me in, depriving me from pursuing all that I was after. Finally, I could take no more frustration and took to the open road again.

About 18 months later, groaning from a horrible hangover in a San Diego apartment after an all-night orgy across the border in Tijuana, Mexico, I knew I had to pull myself together before it was too late. I had just turned 30. I had let my writing go to pot. I was drinking too much. I showed all the little signs of a not-so-quiet desperation. It was time, damnit, to accomplish something more than just the ability to read a Texaco road map or pick out the right girl at a whore house. What I wanted now was a permanent home, a wife, a good job, and the peace of mind that would enable me to begin writing something worth publishing. Moreover, I knew that if any of these things were going to be realized I had better get back to the Middle West where I always felt I truly belonged.

I cannot adequately explain my deep attachment to the "heartland" of America. My mother's people were all born and raised there, and my mother herself was born in Rockford, Illinois. I had been familiar with the Middle Western states since I was 18 years old and every time I returned it was like coming home again. Now, this time I was going to remain and put down some strong roots. My wandering days were going to be over. I decided to settle in the Chicago area, the place where most of my favorite writers — Sandburg, Sherwood Anderson, Masters, Lindsay, Theodore Dreiser, and others — got their start. After a leisurely trip through the northern plains states, including three days in Aberdeen, South Dakota, where I was forced to remain until I could close negotiations for another used car, my old Chevy having died a messy death on the highway outside of town, I chugged to Evanston, Illinois, on October 1, 1958. I rented a third-floor apartment in a big house near Lake Michigan and promptly set up a schedule of writing nights and sleeping days. I had saved some money and knew that if I lived frugally I could avoid the necessity of obtaining employment, for a little while at least.

*   *   *   *   *

I slaved over my writing, spending some long and hard
hours trying to perfect my flabby skills. Before the first year
was out I had placed some poems in a few obscure little
magazines and had married the landlady's daughter. I was
all through with horsing around, you see. Things were start-
ing to fall into place at last. Then, much to my surprise and
delight, some of the better literary quarterlies began accepting my work. I had poems taken by *Prairie Schooner, San
Francisco Review, Minnesota Review, New Mexico Quarterly,* and *Beloit Poetry Journal.* I have made a good beginning,
I thought. I will stay with the poem and see what happens.

*Dave
Etter*

55

DES MOINES

Dave
Etter

This time it's Des Moines
and the wife picks out
a tiny third-floor apartment
right near Drake University
and I get some Iowa plates
for the faithful Plymouth
and buy a guide to the city
and so we're all set
all tucked in
for a long Midwest winter
and I sit here by the heat
on a comfortable davenport
December January February
reading 86 library books
and sucking up bottles
of golden Budweiser
and all the time
the wife is downtown
putting in a busy day
at a hotel switchboard
and March drips into April
and once in a while
I can open a window
and catch a spring breeze
off the Polk County feedlots

But when the wife loses her job
this soft life is over
and we pack the Plymouth again
and go straightway

to her daddy's chicken farm
and she drives 70 80 90 mph
chain-smoking Chesterfields
and saying not a blessed word
and I sprawl in back
and read little magazines
and a stolen copy
of a Rand McNally atlas
and then I count
my library cards
Omaha
Louisville
Sioux Falls
Kansas City
Dayton
Minneapolis
Pittsburgh
New Orleans
Des Moines

. . . .
. . . .

BUNK CAR

Dave
Etter

58

Shoved out on a spur track
across from Petry's Tavern
in East Dubuque
is CB&Q bunk car #212355
salmon colored
peeling curly flakes of paint
muslin curtains at the windows
a tight screen door
a TV antenna jerking in the wind
and a battered kitchen chimney
that looks like a boot gone wrong

Okay now pay attention Clyde
for I'm in pretty bad shape
just bounced out of Petry's
and I have it in my big head
I would like to go railroading
and want to start with a long nap
in old #212355
so can someone
I say can any one of you beer bums
in this here downhill town
fix me up for a stretch on the rails?

PHONE BOOK BLUES

I'm in a smoke-blue town.
Out of money.
Out of gas.   *Dave*
And I'm looking at the phone book.   *Etter*
flipping the phone book pages to   59
Snyder, Albert
Snyder, Bruce K.
Snyder, Daphne
Snyder, Stephen C.
Snyder, Wilma
and your name is not among the Snyder people.
Are you here?
Are you mad?
Are you jailed?
Are you sad?
Or are you pickin' the cabbage
down in Deaf Smith County?
Well, I'm dead in a smoke-blue town.
Yes, I'm a goner now.
Where's the river?
Where's the lake?
Oh where's the water, Wilma Snyder?

TWO DAYS OUT OF THREE CHURCHES

Dave
Etter

60

The Illinois
state trooper
a fresh chaw
of Mail Pouch
swelling
his grizzled jaw
investigates
the abandoned
pickup truck
which
as it turns out
is not abandoned
at all
but two days out
of Three Churches
West Virginia
trouble
is just bound
to come
especially
when you elope
at sixteen
and your
green-eyed
big-dimpled
baby doll
starts to cry
and cry
and you
have to stop
and make her
feel good
all over
again
again

LORCA'S GHOST

Bitter black rain, soft as ashes
stains the cracked tiles
of forgotten towns in Franco's Spain.

Birds with ugly eyes are churched in bells.

Kissed by sick angels,
thin-bellied children curl up in feathers.

Gypsy guitars. The smell of oranges.

Lorca's ghost walks in a grove of bloody moons,
brooding still on a virgin's butchered breasts—
withered blossoms under a thicket of thorns.

The three-cornered hats of the Civil Guard.

Death clatters on the cold stones.
Death breathes in the sour leaves.

MAN TALKING TO HIMSELF

Brown cigars beat green cigars.
You are a fool out of Faulkner,
a farmer finding the general store closed.

Another game? Cut the cards.

She was an old and furious child.
I read that somewhere.

The piano smells like a coffin.

Forget the clinkers, the gone wife.
When the fog lifts we'll go for a spin.

Easy on the Schlitz. Just six cans left.

Let's hear it for matrimony!

AFTER SEEING A PHOTOGRAPH
OF MY GREAT GRANDMOTHER

Dave
Etter

62

Sprawled in the tall grass
after an attic hour
of fumbling among
a trunk of yellowed photographs
I watch a ladybug
crawl across my shiny belly
And again I think of you
in Sangamon County
planting apple trees
in a May Day mist

100 years ago?

Out of this catalpa leaf
and bits of a bluejay's feather
I will make for you now
a summer Valentine
The ladybug flutters
like a tiny heart

Your face cracks
in the china sun

No dont go away

THE GOSPEL SINGER

J. C. Goad, a hard man of God,
fireproofed, Gideon-glazed,
full of pep and Peter,   *Dave*
blows out from the White Star Motel   *Etter*
toward the windy turnpike   63
and Womelsdorf, Pennsylvania.
He is late, as usual,
and his pornographic magazines
flap in the smoky air
in time to radio jazz.
And on the floor,
beside a half-empty bottle
of Southern Comfort,
is a flattened condom
that some wag threw inside
when he stopped at a red light
in Zelienople.

NOVEMBER MOON

Dave
Etter

Cold street is dark and windy.
But moon is hugged by creamy light.
Fried egg in Grandma's skillet.
Halo for prettiest gal in town.

Roger C. Smith still burning leaves.
Smoke curls toward hunter's moon.
Indians dance there in yellow circle.

Rust-orange ring around full moon.
Judge kissing Mrs. Potter's bun.

Wells Fargo of stars.
Big-chested moon man riding shotgun.

Moon: cat's eye before he's hit.

MILES DAVIS

MILES
out of Alton
Illinois
with a horn
between his lips
swings hard through
Two Bass Hit
Straight No Chaser
Ah-Leu-Cha
Well You Needn't
says nothing
all night long
and you know
for sure it's
DAVIS

Dave
Etter

65

THE FIGHTER

Dave
Etter

Nubs Lilly liked to use his fists.
A while back, during a heated discussion
at our fortnightly poker session,
he, as usual, got in the first punch.
But it was also his last one,
because this gas-pump jockey named Sal,
from over in De Kalb County,
quickly laid him out with a left hook.
Later, Nubs had to admit
that he had enough of the fight game
and was not really another up-and-coming
"Two Ton Tony" Galento.

Now it's worse, for he's lifting weights
and talking all the time about Frank Gotch,
Hackenschmidt, and Stanislaus Zbyszco.
He fancies himself a wrestler, you see,
and all his cronies have grown very tired
of being asked to "go a fall or two."
Phil Graham says that if Nubs
keeps on flapping his big yap,
he's going to toss his ass into Illinois Street.
When I tell Nubs this latest bit of news,
he gives me a slow smile and says,
"Strangler" Lilly doesn't like that kind of talk.

BLAKE'S PORCH

The boy with cerebral palsy
has a mop of sandy hair
and round, childlike eyes.

On these bumblebee mornings
they wheel him out for sun
to a porch of potted plants.

Across North Church Street
the old lady has hung
JESUS SAVES on every wall.

Behind her lace curtains
she reads aloud from Kings
and the Acts of the Apostles.

Now the screen door bangs
and she's off again
to cure him with holy words.

The cannibal in his skull
must be devouring
a Congo of missionaries.

They meet once a day.
He knows it's inevitable,
like the next jerk of his head.

MR. FULLER

Dave
Etter

If I could just point to a tractor
out in the cornfield or by the barn
and announce in an authoritative voice,
"Say, there's a Massey-Ferguson 1130:
Perkins direct-injection diesel engine,
turbocharged 120 horsepower,
hydrostatic power-steering,
air-conditioned cab, air-luxe seat, etcetera,"
it might make my mechanically-minded son
sit up and take another look at his old man.

And, if I could go on to proclaim,
ever so casually, you understand,
"Hey, take a gander at the brand new
New Holland 1469 haybine mower-conditioner:
37 horses, water-cooled engine,
and a sicklebar that can cut hay
at 1,520 strokes per minute,"
the boy might even forgive me
for being Webster County's
leading seller of women's clothes.

A DIRTY OLD MAN

Because I have an eye
for the Jewish druggist's buxom wife
who helps out Friday nights
down at the White Star Pharmacy
I buy too much tooth paste
and too many razor blades
and hang around too long pretending
to search for something special
in patent medicines or picture postcards

I'm getting to feel like a horse's ass
but I still look forward to each visit
hoping that the next time I'm there
Mrs. Howard K. Schwartz
will have to bend over to get a bag or box
and I'll be close enough to the action
to grab a good glimpse
of the biggest pair of knockers
this side of the Cumberland Gap

THE RED DEPOT

Dave
Etter

70

Morning fog engulfs the red depot.
I move closer and smell coal smoke.

There are phantoms on the brick platform,
ghosts that rode a lot of varnish.
Sherwood Anderson paces in his old felt hat.
Eugene V. Debs scribbles on an envelope.
Carl Sandburg puffs a stub cigar.

Would you believe it? Would you?

I walk around, getting pretty excited.
A baggage wagon is loaded with sacks of mail.
Eight bankers check giant watches.
The stationmaster sells a ticket to Topeka.

Beyond the water tower, a whistle wails.
Blue rails begin to hum.
Hey, that's it, that's the good music.

I look down the tracks expectantly.
The limited express will be right on time.
But I wait and wait and still no train comes.

Something's wrong. Something is terribly wrong.

Now, the sun burns the fog away.
I am standing in a new parking lot.

The red depot is a long-lost memory.
All the steam lomomotives are gone to scrap.
Most of the engineers and firemen are dead.

There is no one to holler: Alllllll a-board!

BIBLIOGRAPHY

BOOKS

Go Read the River (University of Nebraska Press, 1966)
The Last Train to Prophetstown (University of Nebraska Press, 1968)
Strawberries (Northeast/Juniper Books, 1970)

ANTHOLOGIES AND TEXTBOOKS

America Forever New (Thomas Y. Crowell Co.)
Emily Dickinson: Letters From the World (Corinth Books)
Emily Dickinson: Letters from the World (Corinth Books)
Headway: A Thematic Reader (Holt, Rinehart and Winston, Inc.)
Heartland: Poets of the Midwest (Northern Illinois University Press)
I Love You All Day, It Is That Simple (Abbey Press)
Man in the Poetic Mode 3 (McDougal, Littell & Co.)
Man in the Poetic Mode 4 (McDougal, Littell & Co.)
Ole Anthology (Open Skull Press)
Poetry: Premeditated Art (Houghton Mifflin Co.)
Some Haystacks Don't Even Have any Needle (Scott, Foresman and Co.)
31 New American Poets (Hill and Wang, Inc.)
Voices, An Anthology of Poems and Pictures (Rand McNally & Co.)
Where Steel Winds Blow: Poets on War (David McKay Co.)

SELECTED CRITICAL SOURCES

Beloit Poetry Journal, Summer 1966
Books Abroad, October 1966
Books Today (Chicago Tribune), August 8, 1965
Book Week (Chicago Sun-Times), January 12, 1969
Chicagoland Magazine, November 1968; March 1969
Choice, October 1966
Cronopios, April 1967

Denver Quarterly, vol. 1, no 4, 1967
The Kansas City Star, August 28, 1966
Kayak, No. 7, 1966
Library Journal, July 1966; February 1, 1969
The Madison (Wis.) Capital Times, September 19, 1968
Midwest Quarterly, Winter 1967
New: American & Canadian Poetry, December 1969
Ole, May 1967
Panorama (Chicago Daily News), July 16, 1966
Poetry, February 1967
Quixote, November 1966
The Salt Creek Reader, August 1969
Saturday Review, October 15, 1966
South Florida Poetry Journal, Spring 1970
Western Humanities Review, Winter 1969

LISEL MUELLER

Her first book was published by the University of North Carolina. She is poetry critic for the Chicago *Daily News* and a contributor of essays and poetry to *The New Yorker, Saturday Review,* and *Poetry.*

JOHN KNOEPFLE

About *Rivers into Islands,* published by the University of Chicago Press, Louis Martz said, "This is quiet, understated writing, with the dignity and grace of honest apprehension . . . it has its roots firmly growing in the American grain." *Yale Review,* Spring '66.

*

DAVE ETTER

Writing in *Poetry,* February '67, Etta Blum observes, "In *Go Read the River,* Dave Etter celebrates the place which, for him, is the American Middle West . . . His themes are the homely, daily events: all bounded by the river, the corn fields, and securely within the seasons." Etter has published two books with the University of Nebraska Press. He won the Midland Poetry Award in 1967.

Finished March 1971
450 copies regular, 50 copies special, signed.
Linotype Granjon by The Type House, Minneapolis. Warren's
Olde Style Wove paper, Boston. Hand fed at Sumac Press &
hand bound by Nekola Bindery, La Crosse.
Designed by Emerson G. Wulling

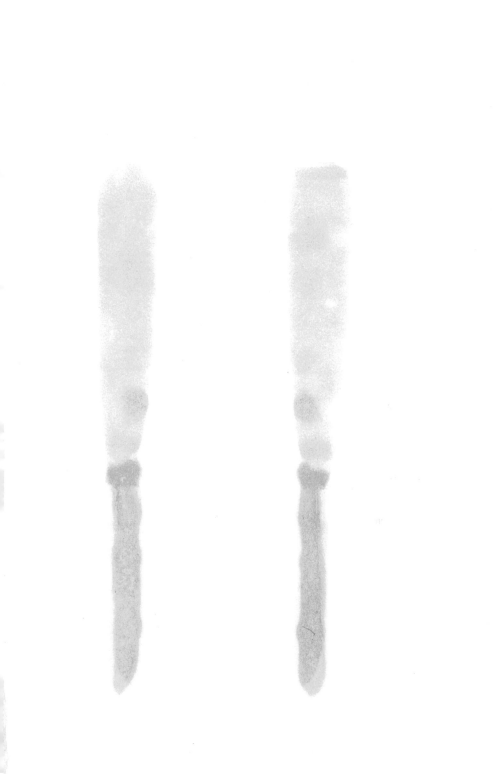

FEB 6 1978

MAY 4 1982